Steel City on Skates: The Pittsburgh Penguins' Journey Through the NHL

Austin Daniel

Published by Austin Daniel, 2023.

While every precaution has been taken in the preparation of this book, the publisher assumes no responsibility for errors or omissions, or for damages resulting from the use of the information contained herein.

STEEL CITY ON SKATES: THE PITTSBURGH PENGUINS' JOURNEY THROUGH THE NHL

First edition. November 23, 2023.

Copyright © 2023 Austin Daniel.

ISBN: 979-8223996392

Written by Austin Daniel.

Also by Austin Daniel

Los Angeles Angels: A Profound Journey through Their Illustrious History
Steel City on Skates: The Pittsburgh Penguins' Journey Through the NHL

Table of Contents

Steel City on Skates: The Pittsburgh Penguins' Journey Through the NHL

The Pittsburgh Penguins: A Decades-Long Journey to Greatness - A Comprehensive History from Inception to Present

The Pittsburgh Penguins have undeniably left an indelible mark on the world of professional ice hockey. Over the course of several decades, this storied franchise has navigated a remarkable journey to greatness, captivating fans with their relentless pursuit of excellence. From their humble beginnings as an expansion team in 1967 to their status as perennial contenders and five-time Stanley Cup champions, the Penguins' evolutionary tale is one that deserves comprehensive exploration. This article takes you on a compelling voyage through time, chronicling every significant milestone and triumph that has shaped the Penguins into the iconic powerhouse they are today. With meticulous detail and expert analysis, we delve into the inception of this esteemed organization, tracing its roots back to its infancy and understanding how it overcame countless obstacles along the way. Strap in for a thrilling retrospective as we relive legendary moments from each era—capturing both breathtaking victories and heart-wrenching defeats—and witness firsthand how brilliant leaders, extraordinary athletes, and unwavering fan support propelled them towards unparalleled success. Whether you're a die-hard Pens enthusiast or simply intrigued by sports history, join us on this enthralling ride through time as we unveil The Pittsburgh Penguins: A Decades-Long Journey to Greatness - A Comprehensive History from Inception to Present like never before seen.

The Birth of the Penguins: From Expansion Team to NHL Contenders

The Pittsburgh Penguins were born in 1967 as part of the National Hockey League's expansion. It wasn't an easy start for the team, facing numerous challenges in their early years. They struggled on the ice, often finishing at or near the bottom of the standings.

However, perseverance paid off for the Penguins. In 1984, they selected a young phenom named Mario Lemieux with the first overall pick in the NHL draft. This marked a turning point for the franchise, as Lemieux would go on to become one of hockey's all-time greats.

With Lemieux leading the way, and bolstered by other talented players like Jaromir Jagr and Marc-Andre Fleury throughout their history, the Penguins transformed from a struggling expansion team into perennial contenders for Lord Stanley's Cup. They have won multiple championships over their storied journey and continue to be a force to be reckoned with in today's NHL.

Building a Foundation: The Early Years of the Penguins Franchise

The Pittsburgh Penguins entered the NHL as an expansion team in 1967. However, it wasn't until the early 1980s that they truly began to establish themselves as a force to be reckoned with.

- In their first decade, the Penguins struggled to find success on the ice. They had several disappointing seasons and faced financial challenges.

- But everything changed when Mario Lemieux, one of hockey's greatest players, was drafted by the team in 1984.

With Lemieux leading the way, the Penguins started to turn things around.

Lemieux quickly made an impact, earning rookie of the year honors and signaling a new era for Pittsburgh hockey. The franchise slowly built a talented roster around him, culminating in back-to-back Stanley Cup championships in 1991 and 1992. These victories solidified their place among NHL powerhouses and set them on course for future greatness.

The Emergence of Super Mario: Mario Lemieux's Impact on the Penguins

- Despite a tumultuous early history, the Pittsburgh Penguins finally found their savior in Mario Lemieux.

- Drafted as the first overall pick in 1984, Lemieux quickly proved himself as a dominant force on the ice.

- With his exceptional scoring ability and smooth skating skills, he transformed the struggling team into contenders.

- Revitalizing a Struggling Franchise:

  - Under Lemieux's leadership, the Penguins went on to win back-to-back Stanley Cup championships in 1991 and 1992.

  - His offensive prowess earned him multiple scoring titles during his career, solidifying his status as one of hockey's greatest players.

- A Legacy of Inspiration:

○ Retiring briefly due to health issues but returning later, Lemieux became an inspiration for many battling cancer or other challenges.

○ Off the ice, he successfully transitioned into ownership of the team and continued guiding them to success.

The Stanley Cup Years: Pittsburgh's First Taste of Glory in the 1990s

In the 1990s, the Pittsburgh Penguins established themselves as a force to be reckoned with in the National Hockey League (NHL). Led by their star player, Mario Lemieux, and supported by a talented roster, the Penguins claimed two Stanley Cup championships during this decade.

Mario Lemieux's Dominance

Mario Lemieux was undoubtedly one of the most influential figures in shaping the success of the Pittsburgh Penguins. Known for his exceptional skill and pure talent on the ice, Lemieux consistently dominated games and amassed impressive statistics. He led not only his team but also stood out among all NHL players as one of history's greatest. With his leadership combined with support from other key players like Jaromir Jagr and Ron Francis, success seemed inevitable for the Penguins.

Back-to-Back Championships

The pinnacle of Pittsburgh's success came when they achieved back-to-back Stanley Cup victories in 1991 and 1992. In these historic seasons, they battled against formidable opponents such as Boston Bruins and Chicago Blackhawks to claim hockey's ultimate prize. These championships solidified their status as an elite team within the NHL.

The remarkable playmaking abilities displayed by Lemieux were central to their triumphs.

The Jagr Era: Dominance and Disappointment

In the 1990s, the Pittsburgh Penguins experienced a period of dominance under the leadership of Jaromir Jagr. Known for his incredible skill and scoring ability, Jagr became the face of the franchise after Mario Lemieux's retirement. With an electrifying offensive lineup that included players like Ron Francis and Kevin Stevens, the Penguins were a force to be reckoned with.

During this era, the team won two consecutive Stanley Cups in 1991 and 1992. They showcased their relentless offense, led by Jagr's dynamic playmaking abilities, which often left opponents struggling to keep up. However, despite their success on the ice, there was also disappointment during this time. Injuries plagued key players like Lemieux and Francis at crucial moments throughout playoff runs.

Despite these setbacks, the Penguins remained a formidable team in the NHL during this decade-long stretch. Their thrilling style of play captivated fans while cementing their status as one of the league's powerhouses. In simple words: The Pittsburgh Penguins dominated hockey in the 1990s led by Jaromir Jagr but faced disappointments due to injuries suffered by key players.

The Lemieux Comeback: A Return to Greatness

After battling through numerous injuries and health issues, Mario Lemieux shocked the hockey world with his comeback in 2000. Despite being away from the game for three-and-a-half years, he quickly picked up where he left off and displayed his unparalleled skill on the ice.

● His return injected a new sense of energy and excitement into Pittsburgh, as fans flocked back to watch their beloved superstar reclaim his spot among hockey's elites.

● Lemieux's leadership qualities were evident as he helped guide a young team towards success, mentoring talented players such as Sidney Crosby along the way.

This incredible comeback solidified Lemieux's status as one of the greatest players to ever grace the sport and reinvigorated both himself and Penguins franchise.

A New Generation: Sidney Crosby and the Next Wave of Penguins Stars

In the early 2000s, a new era began for the Pittsburgh Penguins. Led by their young superstar Sidney Crosby, they embarked on a journey to reclaim their former glory. With his exceptional talent and determination, Crosby quickly became the face of the franchise and started to pave the way for a new generation of Penguins stars.

Alongside Crosby, players like Evgeni Malkin and Kris Letang emerged as key contributors to the team's success. Malkin, with his size and skill, proved to be a formidable force on offense, while Letang showcased his defensive prowess with seamless puck handling and strong instincts.

The trio of Crosby, Malkin, and Letang formed the foundation for what would become one of the most dominant teams in recent NHL history. Their leadership both on and off the ice set a standard for excellence that inspired their teammates to reach new heights. Supported by solid goaltending from Marc-Andre Fleury and later Matt Murray, these young stars led the Penguins to multiple Stanley Cup victories in 2009, 2016, and 2017.

The Arrival of Geno: Evgeni Malkin's Impact on the Penguins

Evgeni Malkin, also known as Geno, made a significant impact on the Pittsburgh Penguins when he joined the team. He was drafted second overall in 2004 and wasted no time showcasing his immense talent on the ice.

With his exceptional scoring ability and playmaking skills, Malkin quickly became one of the league's top players. He formed a dynamic duo with Sidney Crosby, propelling the Penguins to new heights. Together, they led their team to multiple Stanley Cup victories and solidified themselves as an unstoppable force in the NHL.

Malkin's arrival not only elevated the Penguins' performance but also brought a newfound energy to Pittsburgh fans. His ability to create scoring opportunities and make jaw-dropping plays electrified crowds at every game. With each season, Malkin continued to contribute both offensively and defensively, proving himself as an essential player for long-term success.

The Coaching Carousel: From Scotty Bowman to Mike Sullivan

Success with Scotty Bowman

The Penguins' journey to greatness began in 1992 when legendary coach Scotty Bowman led the team to their second Stanley Cup victory. Under his guidance, the Penguins boasted a talented roster that included Mario Lemieux and Jaromir Jagr. With strategic plays and disciplined training, Bowman transformed Pittsburgh into champions.

Turbulent Times

Following their success in the early 90s, the Penguins faced a period of uncertainty as they went through several coaching changes. From Eddie Johnston to Kevin Constantine, each coach brought a different approach but struggled to replicate Bowman's magic. Disappointing playoff runs and inconsistent performances plagued the team during this time.

The Arrival of Mike Sullivan

In 2015, everything changed when Mike Sullivan assumed coaching duties for the Penguins. Known for his no-nonsense approach and emphasis on speed and aggression, Sullivan revitalized the team's playstyle. With Sidney Crosby leading as captain and a refreshed mindset on the ice, Sullivan guided the Penguins to back-to-back Stanley Cups in 2016 and 2017 – solidifying their status as one of hockey's greatest teams.

The Golden Duo: Crosby and Malkin's Dynamic Partnership

Sidney Crosby and Evgeni Malkin form one of the most dynamic partnerships in NHL history. These two players have been instrumental in the success of the Pittsburgh Penguins over the past decade.

A Match Made in Hockey Heaven

Crosby, known for his incredible playmaking abilities, perfectly complements Malkin's goal-scoring prowess. Their chemistry on the ice is unparalleled, with each player almost anticipating where the other will be at any given moment. This telepathic connection has led to countless goals and assists for both players.

Dominating Together

When Crosby and Malkin are on their game, it's nearly impossible to stop them. They feed off each other's energy and elevate their performances to another level. With their combined skill sets, they have set numerous records and won multiple championships for the Penguins.

Their partnership has been a defining characteristic of this team's success throughout its history - from inception up until present day - solidifying their place as one of hockey's all-time greatest duos.

The Rise of Fleury: Marc-Andre Fleury's Journey to Becoming a Penguins Legend

With his lightning-fast reflexes and unwavering determination, Marc-Andre Fleury rose from humble beginnings to become an icon in the world of hockey. Join us as we delve into the captivating story behind this legendary player.

1. Drafted at just 18 years old - In a stroke of fate, the Pittsburgh Penguins selected Fleury first overall in the 2003 NHL Entry Draft. Little did they know that this unassuming teenager would go on to redefine goaltending for generations to come.
2. Overcoming early setbacks - As with any young athlete, there were bumps along the way. Fleury faced criticism and doubts during his rookie season but refused to let them define him. Instead, he honed his skills and embraced every challenge head-on.
3. Three Stanley Cup victories - The mark of greatness is measured by championships won, and Fleury etched his name indelibly into history books by leading the Penguins to three Stanley Cup victories in 2009, 2016, and 2017. His clutch saves propelled his team forward time after time, solidifying his

legacy as one of Pittsburgh's brightest stars.

Fleury may have hung up his skates as a Penguin when he was acquired by Vegas Golden Knights in June 2017 expansion draft; however, his remarkable journey will forever be intertwined with the story of Pittsburgh's rise to greatness.

The Consistency of Excellence: Pittsburgh's Playoff Streak

For over a decade, the Pittsburgh Penguins have established themselves as one of the most consistent and successful franchises in professional hockey. Their streak of consecutive playoff appearances is a testament to their excellence on the ice.

- The Penguins' incredible run began in the 2006-2007 season when they made their first playoff appearance after a six-year drought.

- Led by superstar players like Sidney Crosby and Evgeni Malkin, the team has continued to dominate year after year.

- From 2007 to 2021, the Penguins have clinched a playoff spot every single season.

This remarkable achievement is not just due to individual talent but also reflects upon strong coaching strategies and organizational stability. The team management has consistently made shrewd trades and signings, assembling rosters that are capable of competing for championships. With strong leadership from head coaches such as Dan Bylsma and Mike Sullivan, who guided the team to multiple Stanley Cup victories, there's no doubt that consistency breeds greatness in Pittsburgh.

The Miracle Run: Pittsburgh's Unforgettable 2009 Stanley Cup Victory

After years of ups and downs, the Pittsburgh Penguins finally reached their peak in the 2008-2009 season. Led by superstar forwards Sidney Crosby and Evgeni Malkin, the team embarked on an unforgettable journey to secure their third ever Stanley Cup victory.

- Incredibly talented roster: The Penguins boasted a star-studded lineup that included not only Crosby and Malkin but also veterans such as Sergei Gonchar and Bill Guerin. Their skill, combined with teamwork and determination, proved to be a winning formula.

- Overcoming adversity: The road to glory was not without obstacles. Injuries plagued key players like goaltender Marc-Andre Fleury throughout the playoffs. However, the team rallied together, demonstrating resilience and belief in their abilities.

- Epic playoff battles: Facing formidable opponents such as fierce rivals Washington Capitals and defending champions Detroit Red Wings made each series thrilling. Nail-biting moments showcased Pittsburgh's resolve under pressure while exceptional performances by Crosby and company tilted the scales in their favor.

The culmination of a decades-long pursuit of greatness saw jubilant celebrations across Pittsburgh as the Penguins emerged triumphant against all odds.

The Rebuild and Reinvention: Shaking Up the Penguins Roster

In order to rise from a struggling team in the early 2000s, the Pittsburgh Penguins underwent a major rebuild.

- They traded away high-profile players for draft picks, focusing on building a strong foundation for future success.

- This strategy paid off when they selected Sidney Crosby with the first overall pick in 2005, kickstarting their transformation.

To fully reinvent themselves as contenders, the Penguins also made significant moves to strengthen their roster.

- They acquired key players such as Evgeni Malkin and Marc-Andre Fleury through smart trades and drafting.

- Savy free-agent signings like Chris Kunitz and Pascal Dupuis added invaluable experience to their lineup.

With these changes, the Penguins were able to build a formidable team centered around Crosby and Malkin. Their efforts bore fruit when they won back-to-back Stanley Cups in 2016 and 2017. This remarkable turnaround speaks volumes about the organization's commitment to excellence and constant evolution in pursuit of greatness.

The Back-to-Back Championships: Pittsburgh's 2016 and 2017 Stanley Cup Wins

The Penguins' back-to-back victories in the NHL's Stanley Cup Finals solidified their status as one of hockey's greatest teams. In 2016, led by stars Sidney Crosby and Evgeni Malkin, the Penguins defeated the

San Jose Sharks in a thrilling six-game series to claim their fourth championship in franchise history. The following year, they faced off against the Nashville Predators and once again emerged victorious, winning the cup for a fifth time. These consecutive triumphs marked a remarkable achievement for Pittsburgh.

A Team Effort and Steadfast Determination

Achieving back-to-back championships is no small feat, requiring consistent excellence from every player on the team. The Penguins were successful due to their impressive teamwork and unwavering resolve. Their star-studded roster featured not only Sidney Crosby and Evgeni Malkin but also talented players like Phil Kessel, Kris Letang, Matt Murray, Carl Hagelin, Olli Maatta, Nick Bonino, and Patric Hornqvist.

From stellar goalkeeping by Matt Murray to clutch goals scored by several unlikely heroes throughout both playoffs runs, the Penguins showcased their depth and resilience. This two-year stretch truly cemented them as a force to be reckoned with in NHL history.

The Rise of the Young Guns: Jake Guentzel, Bryan Rust, and the New Generation

With a team history that spans over five decades, it is no surprise that the Pittsburgh Penguins have seen their fair share of talented players. However, in recent years, a new generation of stars has emerged to carry on the franchise's rich legacy. Two key members of this young group are Jake Guentzel and Bryan Rust.

Jake Guentzel burst onto the scene during his rookie season in 2016-2017 with an impressive performance in the playoffs. His knack for scoring timely goals earned him widespread recognition as he became an instrumental part of two Stanley Cup championship runs for the Penguins. Equally as impressive is Bryan Rust who possesses great speed and versatility. Known for his ability to step up in crucial moments, Rust has proven time and again that he is a dependable player.

Together, Guentzel and Rust embody everything that makes this new generation of Penguins special - determination, skillfulness, and a relentless drive to succeed on hockey's biggest stage.

The Coaching Genius: Mike Sullivan's Impact on the Penguins' Success

Since taking over as head coach in 2015, Mike Sullivan has played a pivotal role in the Pittsburgh Penguins' journey to greatness. His coaching prowess and ability to connect with his players have been key factors in the team's continued success.

Sullivan's strategic approach to the game has been instrumental in guiding the Penguins to back-to-back Stanley Cup victories in 2016 and 2017. He emphasizes speed and aggressive play, which has allowed the team to dominate their opponents on both ends of the ice.

Under Sullivan's leadership, players have thrived and reached new heights. He fosters a positive and supportive environment where players are encouraged to take risks and showcase their individual skills. This has resulted in standout performances from superstars like Sidney Crosby and Evgeni Malkin, who have flourished under Sullivan's mentorship.

Overall, Mike Sullivan's impact on the Pittsburgh Penguins cannot be overstated. His coaching genius has transformed an already talented roster into a powerhouse that consistently competes at the highest level of professional hockey.

The Unbreakable Bond: The Connection Between the Penguins and Their Fans

The Pittsburgh Penguins have fostered an unbreakable bond with their devoted fanbase throughout their decades-long journey to greatness.

• A Shared Belief in Perseverance

From the early struggles of the team to its triumphs, fans have remained steadfast supporters through thick and thin. They embody the resilience and determination that define Pittsburgh as a city.

• Game Day Rituals and Camaraderie

Fans' dedication is evident on game days, where they can be seen adorned in team colors, proudly cheering on their beloved Penguins at every opportunity. This sense of camaraderie extends beyond just attending games; it permeates social gatherings, online communities, and even workplace conversations.

• Emotional Rollercoaster of Victories and Defeats

During victories, fans celebrate alongside players as if they were part of the team themselves. Similarly, during defeats or challenging times like injuries or losing streaks - fans collectively share in disappointment but rally behind their players for support.

In conclusion, the enduring connection between the Pittsburgh Penguins and their fans is one built on shared belief in perseverance as well as emotional rollercoasters experienced together during victories or challenges faced by both sides alike.

The Rivalries: Battles with the Flyers, Capitals, and Other Foes

Battles with the Flyers, Capitals, and Other Foes

The Pittsburgh Penguins have had some fierce rivalries over the years. One of their most heated and long-standing rivalries is with the Philadelphia Flyers. These two teams have faced off in intense matchups that often result in physical play and high-scoring games. The rivalry between the Penguins and Flyers dates back to the 1980s when both teams were stacked with talented players.

Another notable rivalry for the Penguins is with the Washington Capitals. This rivalry has intensified in recent years as both teams have been dominant forces in their division. The battles between Sidney Crosby of the Penguins and Alex Ovechkin of the Capitals have captivated fans, making this one of the most exciting matchups in hockey.

In addition to these rivalries, there are other foes that have tested the Penguins' greatness over time. Teams like the New York Rangers and Boston Bruins have provided tough competition for Pittsburgh, pushing them to elevate their game even further. The battles against these formidable opponents showcase just how determined and resilient the Penguins have been throughout their journey to greatness.

The Legacy of Greatness: The Penguins' Lasting Impact on the NHL

The Pittsburgh Penguins have left an indelible mark on the National Hockey League (NHL). Their legacy of greatness is evident in their numerous championships and influential players.

- Championships: With five Stanley Cup championships to their name, including back-to-back wins in 2016 and 2017, the Penguins have established themselves as one of the most successful franchises in NHL history.

● Iconic Players: From Mario Lemieux's skilled finesse to Sidney Crosby's leadership and scoring prowess, the Penguins have boasted some of the game's greatest talents. These players not only achieved personal success but also inspired future generations with their exceptional skills.

● Evolving Style: Beyond individual accomplishments, the Penguins have shaped how hockey is played. Known for their fast-paced, high-scoring style, they revolutionized offensive strategies that influenced teams throughout the league.

A Far-Reaching Impact

The impact of the Pittsburgh Penguins extends beyond just winning games and trophies. They have transformed communities through charitable initiatives and embraced diversity within their organization.

- Community Involvement: Through programs like "Penguins Foundation," they have improved lives by investing in education, healthcare facilities, youth development projects, and environmental causes within Pennsylvania.

- Diversity Advocacy: The franchise has been at the forefront of promoting inclusivity by fostering a welcoming environment for players from diverse backgrounds. They actively support LGBTQ+ initiatives both locally and across all levels of hockey to create a more inclusive sport.

- Inspiring Future Talent: By consistently fielding talented rosters and promoting a winning culture, thePenguins attract young athletes who aspire to reach new heights in ice hockey. Throughout decades, the team's success has motivated aspiring players around North America and beyond.

In conclusion, the Pittsburgh Penguins Legacy goes well-beyond their numerous victories, because it encompasses shaping playing styles, promoting diversity, caring for communities, and leaving a lasting inspiration for future generations.

The Unseen Side of Success: A Glimpse into the Pittsburgh Penguins' Hidden World

In the glamorous world of professional sports, success is often measured by trophies and accolades. Fans cheer on their favorite teams from the stands, marveling at the incredible skill and determination displayed on the field or ice. However, behind every victory lies a hidden world that remains unseen to most - a world of sacrifice, dedication, and perseverance. In this thought-provoking article titled "The Unseen Side of Success: A Glimpse into the Pittsburgh Penguins' Hidden World," we delve deep into the lesser-known aspects of what it truly takes for one team in particular, the esteemed Pittsburgh Penguins hockey franchise, to achieve greatness. Prepare to be captivated as we shed light on these unsung heroes who tirelessly work behind-the-scenes to propel their beloved team towards uncharted heights of triumph.

The Path to the Top: The Penguins' Journey to Success

The Pittsburgh Penguins have long been a force to be reckoned with in the world of ice hockey. But their journey to success has not always been an easy one.

A Team Built on Hard Work and Determination

Behind their countless victories and championships lies a team that is built on hard work and determination. The players push themselves day in and day out, both on and off the ice, to constantly improve their skills and performance. From intense training sessions to strict diets, they leave no stone unturned in their quest for greatness.

Overcoming Challenges Along the Way

But it's not just physical challenges that they have had to overcome. They have also faced adversity both as individuals and as a team. Injuries, slumps in form, and tough losses have tested their resilience time and again. However, instead of giving up or losing hope, they use these setbacks as fuel to come back stronger than ever.

Through persistence, teamwork, and unwavering dedication, the Pittsburgh Penguins have carved out a path towards success that will undoubtedly serve as an inspiration for aspiring athletes around the world.

The Role of Leadership: How Captain Sidney Crosby Guides the Team

Captain Sidney Crosby plays a pivotal role as the leader for the Pittsburgh Penguins. With his strong presence on and off the ice, he ensures that the team functions effectively and achieves success.

- Inspiring motivation: Crosby uses his words and actions to motivate his teammates, pushing them to excel in their performance. He leads by example, showing dedication and determination in every game.

- Effective communication: As captain, Crosby serves as a vital link between players and coaching staff, facilitating smooth communication within the team. This helps in developing strategies and ensuring everyone is on the same page.

- Resilience in challenging times: When faced with setbacks or tough situations, Crosby's leadership shines through. He remains composed under pressure and guides his team towards finding solutions and maintaining focus.

Sidney Crosby's leadership style not only elevates individual performances but also fosters teamwork among players. His ability to inspire motivation, communicate effectively, and remain resilient makes him an invaluable asset to the Pittsburgh Penguins' success.

The Unsung Heroes: The Importance of Supporting Players

The Importance of Supporting Players

In the dazzling world of professional sports, it's easy to focus on the star players who score goals and make incredible saves. However, behind every successful team like the Pittsburgh Penguins, there are unsung heroes: the supporting players. These individuals may not always receive the same recognition as their more celebrated teammates, but their contributions are invaluable.

Supporting players play a crucial role in setting up scoring opportunities for their teammates. They possess excellent passing skills and have a keen understanding of positioning on the ice. By selflessly sacrificing their own statistics for the greater good of the team, they create openings and provide space for their stars to shine.

In addition to assisting offensively, supporting players excel defensively too. They masterfully execute strategy and tactics designed by coaches with precision and dedication. Whether it's blocking shots or successfully killing penalties, these athletes work tirelessly to keep opponents at bay—often without receiving much acknowledgment from fans or media outlets.

By highlighting these unsung heroes' significance in our blog post about hidden aspects contributing to success in hockey exemplified by Pittsburgh Penguins, we aim to shed light on this often-overlooked side of sportsmanship that is vital for teams aiming for long-term victories rather than fleeting moments of individual brilliance.

Behind the Scenes: A Day in the Life of a Pittsburgh Penguins Player

A Day in the Life of a Pittsburgh Penguins Player

Morning Routine

- Players start their day with a nutritious breakfast, focusing on fueling their bodies for optimal performance.

- They arrive at the practice facility early to get in some extra workouts or treatment for any minor injuries.

- Before hitting the ice, players participate in team meetings and watch game footage to strategize and analyze opponents.

Training Sessions

- On ice, players engage in intense drills focused on skating, puck handling, shooting accuracy, and passing skills.

- Strength and conditioning sessions are integral parts of their training routine to build stamina and maintain peak physical condition.

- The coaching staff provides personalized feedback during practice to help players fine-tune their techniques.

Media Obligations

- Throughout the day, players have media obligations such as interviews and promotional shoots that showcase their personalities off the ice.

- These commitments require them to balance professionalism while still connecting with fans through various outlets.

These routines highlight just a glimpse into the behind-the-scenes life of a Pittsburgh Penguins player. From rigorous training sessions to media engagements, every aspect is carefully structured to ensure success on both personal and professional fronts.

The Mental Game: Overcoming Challenges and Staying Focused

The mental game plays a crucial role in the success of the Pittsburgh Penguins. It is not just about physical fitness and skill on the ice; it also involves overcoming challenges and staying focused amidst pressure.

- **Mental resilience**: The players need to be mentally strong to bounce back from setbacks like injuries or losing streaks. They undergo rigorous training to develop their mental toughness, staying positive even when things aren't going well.

- **Focus and concentration**: Hockey requires split-second decisions, so maintaining focus is vital. The team utilizes various techniques such as visualization exercises and mindfulness practices to enhance their concentration during games.

- **Handling pressure**: Playing for one of the top NHL teams brings immense pressure both on and off the ice. To cope with this, players work closely with sports psychologists who help them manage stress, stay calm under intense situations, and make effective choices.

The unseen side of success lies in these mental aspects that contribute greatly to achieving victory for the Pittsburgh Penguins. While fans may primarily focus on physical prowess, it's essential to recognize how much determination, resilience, and psychological strength play a part in their achievements as well.

The Physical Toll: Dealing with Injuries and Recovery

Dealing with Injuries and Recovery

In a demanding sport like ice hockey, injuries are inevitable. The Pittsburgh Penguins have experienced their fair share of injuries throughout the years. It is important to recognize that behind every success story lies a hidden world of physical toll and recovery.

- **Constant Battle:** Injuries can be a constant battle for professional athletes. Whether it's broken bones, torn ligaments, or concussions, each player must face the reality that their body may endure significant damage.

- **Road to Recovery:** Rehabilitation becomes an essential part of an injured player's routine. They work closely with medical professionals to devise specialized treatment plans aimed at regaining strength and mobility.

- **Mental Resilience:** Beyond physical pain, injured players also grapple with mental challenges during their recovery process. Lack of playing time can lead to feelings of frustration and isolation as they watch their teammates compete from the sidelines.

The Pittsburgh Penguins understand the importance of supporting players through these difficult times. By providing them with comprehensive medical care and mental support, they endeavor to help players overcome injuries and get back on the ice stronger than ever before.

Balancing Act: The Challenges of Personal Life and Professional Sports

The Challenges of Personal Life in Professional Sports

- Balancing personal life with the demands of a professional sports career can be incredibly challenging for athletes.

- Athletes often face long and irregular work hours, which can make it difficult to spend quality time with family and friends.

- Frequent travel and training schedules can also take a toll on relationships, forcing players to miss important events or milestones in their loved ones' lives.

The Struggle to Maintain Relationships

- Many athletes find it challenging to maintain romantic relationships due to the demanding nature of their careers.

- Constant travel and time away from home can strain partnerships, leading to feelings of loneliness and isolation.

- Communication is key, but even then, distance can make it hard for athletes to feel fully present in their personal lives while they are on the road competing.

Finding Balance Off the Ice

- To cope with these challenges, many Penguins players prioritize self-care activities such as meditation or spending time outdoors.

- They also rely on support systems within the team and lean on each other for emotional support during tough times.

- Building strong friendships with teammates helps create a sense of camaraderie, making life more enjoyable both on and off the ice.

The Art of Training: Behind the Penguins' Conditioning Regimen

- Intense Workouts

○ Pittsburgh Penguins players undergo rigorous conditioning workouts to maintain peak physical fitness.

○ Exercises such as weight training, cardio drills, and agility work are tailored to each player's specific needs.

○ These intense sessions improve strength, endurance, speed, and overall performance on the ice.

- Nutrition Matters

○ A carefully curated diet plays a crucial role in the Penguins' conditioning program.

○ High-performance meals provide the necessary fuel for their bodies to recover and perform optimally.

○ Nutrient-dense foods like lean proteins, fruits, vegetables, and whole grains are emphasized to support muscle recovery and enhance energy levels.

- Cutting-Edge Technology

○ The use of innovative technology is integrated into the Penguins' training regimen.

○ Advanced tools like heart rate monitors and motion sensors help trainers monitor players' exertion levels and track their progress over time.

○ This data-driven approach enables coaches to design personalized workout plans that maximize each player's potential.

Team Dynamics: Building Camaraderie and Trust

Successful teams don't just excel on the ice - they also build camaraderie and trust off the ice. The Pittsburgh Penguins prioritize teamwork by organizing team-building activities, fostering an environment of open communication, and emphasizing mutual support.

- **Team-building activities:** The Penguins engage in various off-ice activities to strengthen their bond as a team. From bowling nights to charity events, these activities allow players to interact in a relaxed setting and develop personal connections beyond their roles on the ice.

• **Open Communication:** Effective communication is key to building trust within any team. The Penguins encourage all members to speak openly and listen actively, creating an atmosphere where ideas can be freely exchanged without judgment or fear of criticism.

• **Mutual Support:** In order for teammates to trust one another, they must feel supported both on and off the ice. The Penguins exemplify this by showing genuine concern for each other's well-being, offering encouragement during challenging times, and celebrating each other's successes. This culture of mutual support contributes greatly to their success as a cohesive unit.

The Coaching Philosophy: Mike Sullivan's Impact on the Team's Success

A Transformational Leader: Mike Sullivan's Coaching Philosophy

Throughout his tenure as head coach of the Pittsburgh Penguins, Mike Sullivan has been credited with leading the team to multiple championships. His coaching philosophy focuses on fostering a culture of accountability and continuous improvement within the organization.

Prioritizing Team Chemistry and Communication

Sullivan believes that successful teams are built on trust and open communication among players. He emphasizes the importance of forming strong bonds between teammates both on and off the ice. This approach creates a cohesive unit that can effectively work together towards common goals.

To facilitate effective communication, Sullivan encourages his players to express their thoughts and ideas freely. By promoting an inclusive environment where everyone feels heard, he ensures that every player has a voice in shaping team strategies.

Embracing Adaptability and Resilience

Another key aspect of Sullivan's coaching philosophy is embracing adaptability in response to changing game situations or opponents' tactics. He teaches players to be flexible in their approaches so they can adjust quickly during games.

Additionally, resilience is instilled as a core value under Sullivan's guidance. Recognizing that setbacks are inevitable throughout a long season, he empowers his players to bounce back from adversity with determination rather than dwelling on failures.

By focusing on building trust, encouraging communication, embracing adaptability, and fostering resilience, Mike Sullivan has made an indelible impact on the Pittsburgh Penguins' success behind-the-scenes.

The Role of Analytics: How Data Drives the Penguins' Strategies

Data analytics has revolutionized the game of ice hockey, allowing teams like the Pittsburgh Penguins to gain a competitive edge. By analyzing vast amounts of data, the team's front office and coaching staff are able to make informed decisions that drive their strategies on and off the ice.

1. Player Performance Evaluation:

Analytics provides valuable insights into individual player performance, enabling coaches to identify strengths, weaknesses, and areas for improvement. From measuring skating speed to tracking shot accuracy, data allows for objective assessments that go beyond subjective observations.

2. Game Strategy Optimization:

By analyzing historical data on opposing teams and players, as well as past performance against specific opponents or in certain situations (such as power plays), the Penguins can develop effective game strategies customized for each matchup.

3. Injury Prevention:

Using advanced injury prediction models based on player biometrics and gameplay statistics helps prevent injuries by identifying potential risks before they occur. A proactive approach ensures players stay healthy throughout demanding seasons while reducing long-term risks.

In summary, analytics has become an essential tool in shaping successful NHL franchises like the Pittsburgh Penguins'. It empowers decision-makers with actionable insights that enhance player development efforts while fine-tuning strategic approaches needed for consistent success on the ice.

The Influence of Past Legends: The Penguins' Connection to Greats of the Past

The Pittsburgh Penguins have a deep-rooted connection to some of hockey's greatest legends, which has greatly influenced their success. **Mario Lemieux**, widely regarded as one of the best players in NHL history, played his entire career with the Penguins and led them to two Stanley Cup championships during his time as both a player and owner. His impact on the team cannot be overstated.

Another influential figure in Penguins history is **Sidney Crosby**, who followed in Lemieux's footsteps as both captain and superstar player. Crosby, often compared to legendary Wayne Gretzky for his skill set and leadership abilities, has been instrumental in guiding the franchise back to playoff glory with three Stanley Cup wins.

Additionally, past heroes like Jaromir Jagr and Paul Coffey have left lasting legacies that continue to inspire current generations of Penguin players. Their records-breaking performances and indomitable spirit serve as constant reminders that greatness can be achieved through hard work, dedication, and an unwavering commitment to excellence.

A Legacy Fueled by Inspiration

The Pittsburgh Penguins' remarkable success over the years is not simply due to individual talent or skilled coaching; it is also deeply rooted in their ongoing relationship with past legends. By embracing their rich history and learning from those who came before them, each new generation of Pens players carries forward a legacy inspired by greatness.

This unique bond between present-day stars and previous luminaries goes beyond wearing shared colors or playing on the same ice—it instills a sense of responsibility towards upholding tradition while forging new paths towards victory. It is this collective understanding that drives the relentless pursuit for excellence seen amongst every member of the organization—from management down through every player—creating an environment where extraordinary achievements become common practice.

By building bridges across eras—and consistently maintaining connections—the Pittsburgh Penguins not only honor their storied past, but also cultivate an unwavering commitment to success that propels them forward towards new glories.

The Business of Hockey: The Penguins' Impact on the Pittsburgh Community

Economic Boost

- The Pittsburgh Penguins not only excel on the ice but also have a significant impact on the local economy.

• When the team hosts home games, fans flock to downtown Pittsburgh, filling hotels and restaurants and contributing millions of dollars to the city's economy.

• Furthermore, the team's success has led to increased merchandise sales and sponsorships, benefiting local businesses.

Philanthropic Efforts

• Beyond their economic contributions, the Penguins are actively involved in giving back to the community.

• Through their foundation, they support various charitable initiatives such as youth education programs and cancer research.

• Players also regularly visit hospitals and participate in community events, bringing joy to fans and making a lasting difference in people's lives.

The Pressure to Perform: Managing Expectations and Handling Criticism

• High expectations come with success, and the Pittsburgh Penguins are no exception. With back-to-back Stanley Cup wins in 2016 and 2017, the pressure on the team to perform at a high level is intense.

• Players face constant scrutiny from fans, media, and even their own teammates. Every mistake or loss is analyzed and criticized. This constant pressure can take a toll on their mental health and well-being.

- To manage these expectations, players rely on various coping strategies such as positive self-talk, visualization techniques, and seeking support from teammates and mental health professionals.

Dealing with Criticism

- Criticism comes with the territory of being a professional athlete. Players have to learn how to handle it constructively without letting it affect their performance.

- The Penguins organization provides resources for players to develop resilience skills and deal with criticism effectively. This includes workshops focused on building self-confidence, effective communication skills, and emotional regulation techniques.

- It's important for players to filter out unwarranted negativity from constructive criticism. They focus on learning from their mistakes rather than dwelling on them, allowing them to continually improve their game.

(134 words)

The Penguin Way: The Team's Unique Culture and Traditions

The Pittsburgh Penguins have cultivated a unique culture that sets them apart from other NHL teams. This culture is built on values such as teamwork, perseverance, and dedication. From the moment a player steps foot in their locker room, they become part of a tight-knit family that supports each other both on and off the ice.

One of the team's most cherished traditions is their pre-game ritual known as "The Circle." Before every game, players form a circle on the ice where they share words of encouragement and support for one another. This tradition not only helps to build camaraderie but also serves as a reminder of the importance of unity and trust within the team.

Another aspect of Penguin culture revolves around respect for veterans. Younger players are expected to show deference to those who have been with the team for longer periods, acknowledging their experience and leadership. This emphasis on respecting elders has helped foster an environment of mentorship within the organization, allowing younger talent to learn from seasoned veterans.

With its strong emphasis on teamwork, rituals like "The Circle," and respect for veteran leadership, it becomes evident why this unique culture plays such an integral role in fostering success for the Pittsburgh Penguins year after year. Their commitment to these traditions unifies individuals into one cohesive unit focused on achieving greatness together.

From Draft to Ice: The Penguins' Player Development System

The Pittsburgh Penguins have a carefully structured player development system that brings promising young talent from the draft to the ice.

- **Step 1: Assessing Potential** Before drafting players, the Penguins' scouting team thoroughly evaluates their potential. They consider factors such as skill level, hockey intelligence, and physical attributes.

- **Step 2: Individualized Development Plans** Once drafted, each player is assigned an individualized development plan tailored to their specific needs. This plan includes on-ice training sessions, off-ice workouts, and guidance from experienced coaches.

- **Step 3: AHL Progression** Players typically start their professional careers in the American Hockey League (AHL), where they continue to hone their skills under close supervision. Here they gain valuable experience while adjusting to the faster pace of pro-level play.

With this systematic approach and commitment to developing talented individuals, it's no wonder why the Pittsburgh Penguins have become perennial contenders in professional hockey.

The Role of Technology: Innovations in Training and Performance Analysis

Technology in Training

Technology plays a vital role in the training and performance analysis of the Pittsburgh Penguins. The team utilizes cutting-edge tools and equipment to maximize their efficiency on the ice. One such technology is virtual reality, which allows players to simulate game scenarios and reinforce their decision-making skills. This immersive training experience gives them an edge over their opponents.

Performance Analysis with Data

Data-driven analysis has become an integral part of sports, and the Penguins are no exception. They use advanced analytics software to analyze player performance, identify strengths, weaknesses, and areas for improvement. These insights enable coaches to develop customized training programs that target specific skills or tactics. By incorporating data into their decision-making process, the Penguins are able to enhance both individual and team performance.

Wearable Technology

Wearable technology also plays a significant role in optimizing player performance. Devices like heart rate monitors and GPS trackers provide real-time information on players' physical condition during games and practices. This data helps trainers tailor workouts tailored specifically towards each player's needs while reducing the risk of injuries caused by overexertion.

Overall, technology has revolutionized how sports teams like the Pittsburgh Penguins train and analyze performances. With its wide range of applications - from virtual reality training to advanced data analysis - technology continues to push boundaries in uncovering the hidden side of success for professional athletes.

The Traveling Circus: Life on the Road for the Pittsburgh Penguins

Life on the Road with the Pittsburgh Penguins

Traveling is a way of life for the Pittsburgh Penguins. With months spent away from home, they become a tight-knit group on and off the ice.

- The players spend countless hours traveling to different cities to compete in games.

- They are constantly adjusting their schedules and routines to accommodate different time zones.

- Long flights and hotel stays become second nature as they navigate through grueling road trips.

Challenges of Constant Travel

Life on the road can present various challenges for the Penguins:

1. Fatigue: The constant travel and lack of routine can lead to exhaustion for both players and staff members.
2. Away from loved ones: Spending extended periods away from family and friends is emotionally taxing.
3. Pressure of performance: Playing in unfamiliar arenas adds an extra layer of pressure to perform well.

Building Camaraderie amidst the Trials

Despite these challenges, there are positive aspects that come with life on the road:

1. Bonding opportunities: Time spent traveling together fosters strong camaraderie among teammates.
2. Unique experiences: Exploring new cities during downtime provides exciting cultural experiences that enrich their lives beyond hockey.

By understanding this unseen side of success, fans gain insight into what it takes for professional athletes like the Pittsburgh Penguins to excel while living a nomadic lifestyle throughout their season journey.

Philanthropy and Giving Back: The Penguins' Charitable Initiatives

Making a Difference in the Pittsburgh Community

The Pittsburgh Penguins have made it a priority to give back to their community. Through various charitable initiatives, they are making a difference in the lives of those in need. Their commitment to philanthropy is an unseen side of their success that deserves recognition.

Helping Children Get the Education They Deserve

One area where the Penguins focus their efforts is on education. They understand the importance of providing children with access to quality education and resources. Through programs like "Pens Foundation," they support schools, libraries, and literacy programs in underserved areas, ensuring that every child has a chance at success.

Supporting Local Nonprofit Organizations

In addition to education, the Penguins also lend a helping hand to local nonprofit organizations. By partnering with these organizations, they provide assistance for various causes such as homelessness, hunger relief, and healthcare services. Their contributions help improve the lives of countless individuals within their community.

Overall, the charitable initiatives undertaken by the Pittsburgh Penguins demonstrate their dedication to giving back and making a positive impact off the ice. These unseen acts are just as important as their accomplishments on game day and deserve recognition for their role in creating a better future for those in need.

The Legacy of Success: Pittsburgh Penguins' Impact on the NHL

The Pittsburgh Penguins have left an indelible mark on the National Hockey League (NHL).

- With their consistent success, they have become a model franchise for other teams to emulate.

- Their winning ways and dedication to excellence have influenced the league as a whole.

Elevating the Level of Play

The Penguins' style of play has had a significant impact on how hockey is played in today's NHL.

- Known for their speed, skill, and creativity, they have inspired other teams to adopt a more up-tempo and offensive-minded approach.

- This has led to more exciting games and increased scoring throughout the entire league.

Developing Young Talent

One area where the Penguins truly excel is in player development.

- Their ability to identify and nurture young talent has allowed them to consistently replenish their roster with skilled players.

- As a result, they have been able to maintain their competitive edge year after year.

Overall, the success of the Pittsburgh Penguins goes beyond just wins and championships. They have forever changed the landscape of hockey by elevating the level of play and setting new standards for player development in the NHL.

The Evolution of Greatness: From Mario Lemieux to Sidney Crosby and Evgeni Malkin – A Tale of Pittsburgh Penguins' Legacy

The Pittsburgh Penguins have long been regarded as a dominant force in the National Hockey League (NHL), and their success can be attributed to the remarkable evolution of greatness within their ranks. From the iconic Mario Lemieux to the modern-day stars Sidney Crosby and Evgeni Malkin, this article delves into the captivating tale of how these exceptional players have built a legacy for the Penguins, transforming them into true contenders year after year. Through an exploration of their individual journeys, undeniable skillsets, and impact on the team's achievements, we unearth a fascinating narrative that resonates with fans and cements the Penguins' place in hockey history. Brace yourself for an enthralling account that showcases not only how talent evolved but also

how it laid down a foundation for continued greatness within one of
NHL's most storied franchises - The Pittsburgh Penguins.

Mario Lemieux: The Beginnings of Greatness

Mario Lemieux, a native of Montreal, Canada, began his journey to
greatness at just five years old. It was during the annual Canadian pond
hockey tournament that young Mario first showcased his incredible skills
on the ice.

At 14 years old, Lemieux joined the prestigious Laval Voisins junior team
and quickly became a standout player. Scouts from NHL teams were
awed by his natural talent and exceptional scoring ability. In 1984, at
only 18 years old, he was selected as the first overall pick in the NHL
draft by none other than the Pittsburgh Penguins.

Lemieux's impact on the Penguins was immediate and undeniable. He
wasted no time in proving himself as an elite player in the league,
winning Rookie of the Year honors with an impressive 100-point season.
With each passing year, his skillset continued to evolve and mature -
from powerful skating to impeccable stickhandling - solidifying him as
one of hockey's greatest players.

Mario Lemieux's Impact on the Penguins' Legacy

Mario Lemieux, a legendary figure in NHL history, played an
instrumental role in shaping the Pittsburgh Penguins' legacy.

- Transforming a Struggling Franchise: When Lemieux
joined the Penguins as the first overall pick in 1984, the team
was floundering both on and off the ice. However, his
exceptional skills and leadership revitalized the organization.

He was able to reverse its fortunes by leading them to two consecutive Stanley Cup championships in 1991 and 1992.

● Resilience Despite Health Challenges: Not only did Lemieux exhibit unparalleled talent, but he also defied incredible odds by returning to play after being diagnosed with Hodgkin's lymphoma. His determination inspired his teammates and fans alike, solidifying his place as an iconic figure who brought hope to Pittsburgh.

● Unprecedented Performance: Lemieux earned numerous accolades throughout his career, including six Art Ross Trophies for leading scorers and three Hart Trophies for Most Valuable Player. His impressive stats continue to stand among hockey's elite even years after his retirement.

By leaving such a profound impact on both on and off the ice during his tenure with the Penguins, Mario Lemieux helped set a foundation of greatness that paved the way for future generations of players—including Sidney Crosby and Evgeni Malkin—to carry forward.

The Artistry of Lemieux's Playmaking Abilities

Mario Lemieux possessed incredible playmaking skills that set him apart from other players in the NHL. His vision on the ice was unparalleled, allowing him to anticipate plays and make precise passes with ease. With his exceptional stickhandling and skating abilities, he could effortlessly maneuver through defenders to create scoring opportunities for himself and his teammates.

Lemieux had a knack for finding open spaces on the ice, often making smart positional decisions that allowed him to quickly move into advantageous positions. His ability to read plays and exploit gaps in the defense made it difficult for opponents to contain him. Whether it was a saucer pass over multiple players or a behind-the-back feed through traffic, Lemieux's creativity knew no bounds.

His patience with the puck was another aspect of his game that impressed fans and analysts alike. Lemieux would often hold onto the puck just long enough for an opening to appear before delivering a pinpoint pass or unleashing his deadly shot on goal. This composure under pressure was crucial in tight games and helped elevate his team's performance in critical moments.

Overall, Mario Lemieux's playmaking abilities were truly remarkable, leaving a lasting impact on both Penguins' history and hockey as a whole.

Lemieux's Battle with Cancer and His Return to Greatness

In the midst of his illustrious career, Mario Lemieux faced a harrowing battle with cancer. Diagnosed with Hodgkin's lymphoma in 1993, he made the courageous decision to take a leave from professional hockey for treatment. Despite this setback, Lemieux displayed unwavering determination and strength throughout his recovery.

After undergoing radiation therapy and intense chemotherapy sessions, Lemieux not only beat cancer but also defied all odds by returning to the ice. In an inspiring comeback that stunned fans and experts alike, he resumed his dominance in the sport he loved so dearly. This chapter in his life solidified him as more than just an incredible athlete – it established him as a symbol of perseverance and resilience.

Sidney Crosby: The Next Generation of Greatness

While Mario Lemieux may have paved the way for greatness in Pittsburgh, it is Sidney Crosby who has taken that torch and run with it.

● With his incredible skill set and unwavering determination, Crosby has solidified himself as one of the best players to ever lace up a pair of skates.

● From a young age, he displayed an uncanny ability to control the game, making his teammates better while simultaneously dominating opponents.

● Unlike many star athletes, Crosby never let success go to his head; instead, he continued to work tirelessly on improving his skills both on and off the ice.

Crosby's leadership both on and off the ice sets him apart from other players.

● He leads by example with relentless effort during games and dedication in practices.

● Off the ice, he takes time to give back through charitable endeavors that make a meaningful impact in communities across North America.

● His tireless work ethic serves as an inspiration not only to aspiring hockey players but also anyone striving for excellence in their respective fields.

Sidney Crosby is not just another great player; he represents the evolution of greatness within Pittsburgh Penguins' legacy.

Crosby's Rise to Stardom and Leadership Qualities

Crosby's Rise to Stardom

Sidney Crosby, widely regarded as one of the greatest hockey players of his generation, began his journey to stardom at a young age. Hailing from Cole Harbour, Nova Scotia, he displayed remarkable talent and determination on the ice. At just 16 years old, he was already being hailed as an exceptional player with unlimited potential.

Crosby's skill set was undeniable; his speed, agility, and puck-handling abilities were unmatched. His dedication to honing his skills through rigorous training routines allowed him to continuously improve and evolve as a player. With every game he played, Crosby proved himself worthy of the high expectations placed upon him.

Leadership Qualities

Not only did Crosby possess exemplary athletic abilities, but he also demonstrated outstanding leadership qualities that set him apart from his peers. From a young age, he exhibited maturity beyond his years and led by example both on and off the ice.

Crosby's work ethic served as an inspiration for teammates who admired his dedication and unwavering commitment to success. He had the ability to rally those around him during crucial moments in games with motivating speeches or by displaying exceptional performance under pressure.

His humility also contributed to inspiring others; despite achieving numerous personal accolades throughout his career, Crosby always emphasized team success over individual accomplishments. This selflessness created a culture within the Pittsburgh Penguins organization focused on unity and collective goals rather than individual glory.

The Unforgettable "Golden Goal" and Crosby's Olympic Success

Sidney Crosby cemented his status as a hockey legend with his unforgettable performance at the 2010 Winter Olympics in Vancouver. The tension was palpable as Canada faced off against the United States in the final, and it all came down to overtime. In a sublime display of skill, Crosby scored the game-winning goal that will forever be etched in Canadian hockey history. This moment - dubbed the "golden goal" - not only secured Canada's victory but also showcased Crosby's ability to thrive under pressure.

Crosby's success at the Olympics didn't end there. Four years later, he once again led Team Canada to gold at the 2014 Winter Olympics in Sochi. His playmaking abilities and leadership on and off the ice were instrumental in securing another Olympic triumph for his country. With two Olympic gold medals under his belt, Sidney Crosby solidified his position as one of hockey's most accomplished players.

Key Points:

- Sidney Crosby scored an iconic "golden goal" during overtime at the 2010 Winter Olympics.

- His performance demonstrated his ability to rise to big moments.

- He went on to lead Team Canada to another gold medal four years later.

- His contributions both on and off the ice established him as a true leader within international hockey circles.

Crosby's Injury Setbacks and Resilience

- Sidney Crosby has faced numerous injury setbacks throughout his career but has displayed remarkable resilience in overcoming them.

- In 2011, Crosby suffered a concussion that kept him out of action for almost a year, raising concerns about the impact on his playing abilities.

- Despite this setback, he made an impressive comeback in 2012 by leading the Penguins to the playoffs with his exceptional skills and determination.

Evgeni Malkin: The Russian Sensation

Evgeni Malkin emerged as a hockey superstar after being drafted by the Pittsburgh Penguins in 2004.

- Born in Russia, Malkin showed immense talent and was quick to make his mark on the ice.

- His incredible skills and exceptional playmaking abilities earned him numerous accolades throughout his career.

Malkin's impact on the team and the league cannot be overstated:

- With his powerful shot and strategic puck handling, he became an essential part of the Penguins' offense.

- In 2009, he played a pivotal role in leading the team to win their third Stanley Cup championship.

- Over the years, Malkin has consistently been one of the league's top scorers, cementing himself as one of Pittsburgh's most beloved players.

Despite some injuries that have plagued him during certain seasons, Malkin continues to show resilience on and off the ice:

- His dedication to training and passion for the game are evident in each performance.

• As he carries forward Mario Lemieux's legacy alongside Sidney Crosby, there is no doubt that Evgeni Malkin is a vital piece of Pittsburgh Penguins' history.

Malkin's Dynamic Playing Style and Offensive Prowess

Evgeni Malkin has long been recognized as one of the most dynamic players in the NHL. With lightning-fast speed, agility, and impressive stickhandling skills, Malkin possesses a playing style that keeps opponents on their toes. His ability to change direction quickly combined with his powerful shot make him a constant threat on the ice.

Malkin's offensive prowess is evident from his impressive stat line year after year. He consistently ranks among the league leaders in points, goals, and assists. His ability to create scoring opportunities for himself and his teammates sets him apart from others in the game.

- Strong skating abilities

- Exceptional puck control

- Quick decision-making

- Accurate shooting accuracy

When watching Malkin play, it is clear that he approaches each game with intensity and a desire to win. Whether it's making pinpoint passes or finding open space to take a shot on net, Malkin plays with an unmatched level of skill and determination. As an integral part of the Pittsburgh Penguins' legacy alongside Lemieux and Crosby, Malkin has solidified his place as one of the greats in NHL history through his dynamic playing style and offensive prowess.

Malkin's Contributions to the Penguins' Championship Wins

One significant aspect of the Pittsburgh Penguins' legacy lies in Evgeni Malkin's contributions to their multiple championship wins.

1. Consistency and Skill: Known for his exceptional skills, Malkin consistently delivered high-quality performances throughout his career with the Penguins. His ability to control the puck and create scoring opportunities has made him a vital part of the team's offensive success.

2. Playoff Dominance: Malkin's impact on the Penguins is particularly evident in playoff games. He has consistently elevated his play during crucial moments, often leading the team in points scored during playoff runs.

3. Team player mentality: Despite being incredibly talented individually, Malkin understands that hockey is a team sport. He values teamwork and frequently assists fellow players, making him an important asset in creating synergy among teammates.

The combination of consistent skill, playoff dominance, and a team player mentality has contributed significantly to Evgeni Malkin's integral role in the Pittsburgh Penguins' journey towards greatness over the years

The Crosby-Malkin Duo: A Match Made in Hockey Heaven

The Pittsburgh Penguins have been fortunate enough to witness the dynamic duo of Sidney Crosby and Evgeni Malkin dominating the ice for well over a decade. With their exceptional skills, hockey IQ, and chemistry on the ice, they have become one of the most formidable pairs in NHL history.

Their individual talents perfectly complement each other. Crosby is known for his incredible playmaking abilities and vision on the ice, always finding ways to set up his teammates with pinpoint passes. Malkin, on the other hand, brings raw power and an arsenal of offensive moves that make him almost impossible to defend against.

When these two superstars team up, magic happens. Their ability to anticipate each other's next move allows them to create scoring chances out of thin air - something that fans never tire of witnessing. Whether it's Crosby setting up Malkin for a stunning goal or vice versa, their partnership has produced countless highlight-reel moments over the years.

Key Takeaways:

- Sidney Crosby and Evgeni Malkin form one of the greatest duos in NHL history.

- They complement each other perfectly with their unique skills.

- The chemistry between them allows them to create unforgettable plays on the ice.

The Impact of Lemieux's Mentorship on Crosby and Malkin

Lemieux's Mentorship: A Guiding Light for Crosby and Malkin

Lemieux's mentorship has undeniably had a profound impact on the development and success of both Sidney Crosby and Evgeni Malkin.

- From the moment Crosby entered the league as an 18-year-old rookie, he was thrust into the spotlight. However, with Lemieux by his side as a mentor and role model, he was able to navigate the pressures and expectations with grace and determination.

- Likewise, for Malkin, who joined the Penguins in 2006, having Lemieux as a guiding force provided invaluable support. He looked up to Mario's distinguished career and relied on his experience to navigate challenges both on and off the ice.

Sharing Wisdom: Lessons Passed Down from Mentor to Protégés

Lemieux shared his wisdom with Crosby and Malkin through actions that spoke louder than words.

- He taught them about teamwork by leading by example during practices, displaying relentless work ethic day in and day out.

- Furthermore, Lemieux emphasized perseverance when facing adversity. His own battles against illness showed them that setbacks were merely stepping stones towards future victories.

Overall, Lemieux's involvement in their lives molded not only two of hockey's greatest players but also instilled in them important values that will forever be part of their legacy.

The Penguins' Dynasty: Lemieux, Crosby, and Malkin

The Pittsburgh Penguins have experienced an unparalleled dynasty with the arrival of Mario Lemieux, Sidney Crosby, and Evgeni Malkin.

- **Mario Lemieux:** Lemieux's impact on the Penguins organization cannot be overstated. As one of the greatest players in NHL history, he led the team to back-to-back Stanley Cup victories in 1991 and 1992. Despite his battles with injuries throughout his career, he managed to win numerous awards and cement himself as a legend in Pittsburgh.

- **Sidney Crosby**: After years of struggles following Lemieux's retirement, the Penguins got another generational talent in Sidney Crosby. His exceptional skills combined with his natural leadership ability made him a vital asset to the team. Under his captaincy, the Penguins achieved three Stanley Cup championships in 2009, 2016, and 2017.

- **Evgeni Malkin**: A dynamic force alongside Crosby is Evgeni Malkin. With his powerful shot and incredible playmaking abilities, Malkin has been an integral part of the Penguins' success over the years. He played a significant role in winning three Stanley Cups with Pittsburgh alongside Crosby.

The trio of Lemieux, Crosby, and Malkin has propelled the Penguins to new heights of greatness by establishing a strong legacy within the franchise's history while also inspiring future generations of hockey players to strive for excellence.

The Evolution of the Penguins' Style of Play Under Lemieux, Crosby, and Malkin

Under Lemieux:

Mario Lemieux revolutionized the Penguins' style of play by showcasing his exceptional skill and finesse on the ice. With his innate vision and creativity, he brought a new level of excitement to the team's offensive strategy. His ability to control the game flow and make precise passes enabled him to set up his teammates for scoring opportunities.

Lemieux's influence extended beyond offense, as he also emphasized strong defensive play. He prioritized backchecking and disciplined positioning, leading by example in both ends of the rink. This commitment to well-rounded hockey helped transform the Penguins into a formidable force during his tenure.

Crosby-Malkin Era:

The arrival of Sidney Crosby and Evgeni Malkin ushered in a new era for Pittsburgh hockey – one marked by relentless speed, tenacity, and an emphasis on puck possession. Their playing styles complemented each other perfectly: while Crosby showcased great finesse with extraordinary stickhandling skills, Malkin's physicality added power behind every move.

Under their leadership, the Penguins adopted an aggressive forechecking strategy designed to create turnovers quickly and generate high-scoring chances through continuous pressure on opponents. The duo thrived in transition plays as they utilized their speed to exploit gaps in opposing defenses while maintaining excellent support from their linemates.

In addition to their offensive prowess, both Crosby and Malkin demonstrated improved defensive responsibility throughout their careers; they understood that preventing goals was just as crucial as scoring them. By embracing a two-way approach under these superstars' guidance, Pittsburgh has maintained its reputation for being competitive at both ends of the ice.

The Legacy of Greatness: How Lemieux, Crosby, and Malkin Have Shaped the Penguins' Franchise

Mario Lemieux's arrival in Pittsburgh marked a turning point for the Penguins' franchise. His exceptional skill and leadership transformed them into contenders. With his offensive prowess and ability to rally his teammates, Lemieux led the team to two Stanley Cup championships in 1991 and 1992. He left an indelible mark on the organization as one of the greatest players in NHL history.

Following in his footsteps, Sidney Crosby emerged as a new face of greatness for the Penguins. Nicknamed "The Next One," Crosby displayed immense talent from an early age. His remarkable hockey IQ and scoring touch propelled him to become one of the league's top players. Under Crosby's captaincy, Pittsburgh celebrated three more Stanley Cup victories – in 2009, 2016, and 2017 – solidifying their status as perennial contenders.

Evgeni Malkin has been another key figure in shaping the legacy of greatness within the Penguins' franchise. As much as he excels individually with his powerful shots and playmaking abilities, Malkin also thrives when playing alongside Crosby. Together they form a formidable duo that consistently poses challenges for opposing teams' defenses. With their combined efforts over the years, Malkin has contributed crucially to Pittsburgh's success by earning multiple All-Star selections and winning accolades such as playoff MVP.

The trio of Lemieux, Crosby, and Malkin not only brought individual brilliance but also established a culture of excellence within the Penguins organization that continues today. Their impact extends beyond statistics; it lies within inspiring future generations with their passion for both team success and personal growth on ice.

The Penguins' Success Beyond the Trio: The Importance of Supporting Cast

The Importance of Supporting Cast

A team's success in hockey is not solely dependent on its star players. While the Pittsburgh Penguins have undoubtedly been fortunate to have Mario Lemieux, Sidney Crosby, and Evgeni Malkin leading the way for them over the years, their supporting cast has played a crucial role in their achievements.

1. Consistent contributions: The Penguins' supporting cast has consistently provided valuable contributions throughout their journey to greatness. From reliable goal scorers to dependable defenders, these players have stepped up when needed and helped maintain the team's momentum during key moments in games.
2. Depth and versatility: A strong supporting cast adds depth and flexibility to a team's lineup. By having capable players who can seamlessly fill various roles, whether it be as an offensive sparkplug or a shutdown defenseman, the Penguins have been able to adapt their game plan based on opponent strategies or player injuries.
3. Mentoring younger talent: Along with on-ice performance, veterans within the supporting cast help mentor and nurture younger talent within the organization. Their experience and knowledge provide guidance both on and off the ice, helping future stars develop into formidable assets for the team.

In conclusion, while superstars like Lemieux, Crosby, and Malkin draw much attention for their extraordinary skills, it is important not to overlook the significance of a strong supporting cast. These unsung heroes bring consistency, depth, versatility, and mentorship that complement the talents of star players – ultimately contributing to sustained success for teams like the Pittsburgh Penguins.

The Penguins' Impact on the City of Pittsburgh and Hockey Culture

The Pittsburgh Penguins have had a profound impact on both the city of Pittsburgh and hockey culture as a whole.

- Economic Boost: With their success, the Penguins have brought economic prosperity to Pittsburgh. Hosting games at PPG Paints Arena draws in thousands of fans from near and far, contributing to local businesses such as restaurants, hotels, and shops.

- Strengthening Community Spirit: As a beloved sports team, the Penguins have united the people of Pittsburgh. Their victories bring joy and pride to the community, fostering a strong sense of camaraderie among fans who gather together to support their team.

- Inspiring Young Players: Superstars like Mario Lemieux, Sidney Crosby, and Evgeni Malkin have inspired countless young players in Western Pennsylvania to pursue their own dreams of playing professional hockey. The Penguins' legacy has created a lasting impact on youth hockey programs in the area.

Overall, through their achievements on ice and off it's clear that the Penguins are more than just an incredible hockey team—they are an integral part of what makes Pittsburgh great.

The Penguins' Rivalries and Memorable Playoff Moments

Rivalries and Playoff Greatness

Fierce Rivalries:

Throughout their legacy, the Penguins have had intense rivalries with several teams. The most noteworthy rivalry has been with the Philadelphia Flyers, known as the "Battle of Pennsylvania." These showdowns have featured hard-hitting action and high-scoring games that electrify fans on both sides.

Another notable rivalry is with the Washington Capitals. This fierce rivalry intensified in the playoffs, where epic battles between superstar players like Crosby and Ovechkin have created unforgettable moments.

Memorable Playoff Moments:

The Penguins' playoff history is filled with memorable moments that have solidified their greatness. One standout moment came during the 1991 Stanley Cup Finals when Mario Lemieux showcased his skill by scoring an unprecedented five goals in a single game against the Minnesota North Stars.

In more recent years, Evgeni Malkin's performance during the 2009 playoffs cannot be overlooked. With his exceptional playmaking abilities, Malkin propelled Pittsburgh to victory, earning him the distinction of being named MVP of those playoffs.

Additionally, Sidney Crosby's iconic overtime goal in game two of the 2016 Stanley Cup Finals against San Jose Sharks will always be remembered as one of his defining playoff moments. Crosby's determination and skill were on full display as he netted this crucial game-winning goal that ultimately led to another championship for Pittsburgh.

The Future of Greatness: The Penguins' Legacy Continues with the Next Generation

While Mario Lemieux, Sidney Crosby, and Evgeni Malkin have left an indelible mark on the Pittsburgh Penguins franchise, their legacy is not confined to their playing days. As these iconic players near the twilight of their careers, a new generation has emerged to carry on the tradition of greatness in Pittsburgh.

A New Crop of Talented Stars Rises

The Penguins organization has done an exceptional job at nurturing young talent and developing them into future superstars. Names like Jake Guentzel, Bryan Rust, and Kasperi Kapanen have already shown immense promise and have been vital contributors to the team's continued success.

Stanley Cup Dreams With a Fresh Batch

With this new influx of talented individuals comes renewed hope for another Stanley Cup win. While it will undoubtedly be challenging to fill the void left by legends like Lemieux and Crosby, there is no shortage of determination within this next generation to bring home hockey's ultimate prize once again.

Don't miss out!

Visit the website below and you can sign up to receive emails whenever Austin Daniel publishes a new book. There's no charge and no obligation.

https://books2read.com/r/B-A-IQJBB-QSBRC

BOOKS 2 READ

Connecting independent readers to independent writers.

Did you love *Steel City on Skates: The Pittsburgh Penguins' Journey Through the NHL*? Then you should read *Pittsburgh Steelers Fun Facts*[1] by Trivia Ape!

[2]

Discover the ultimate fan experience with the "Pittsburgh Steelers Fun Facts" book – an exciting journey through the rich history and legendary moments of this iconic NFL team. Packed with over 1000 detailed fun facts, this family-friendly book is designed to challenge and entertain fans of all ages while deepening their knowledge of the Pittsburgh Steelers.

Immerse yourself in the heart-pounding action, unforgettable plays, and standout players that have defined their legacy. From thrilling rivalries and historic divisional matchups to legendary offensive star

---

1. https://books2read.com/u/mYqyLV

2. https://books2read.com/u/mYqyLV

players and iconic stadium facts, each question provides a captivating glimpse into the team's remarkable journey.

Unearth captivating insights into the team origins, relive iconic victories, and celebrate the achievements of Hall of Fame players who have graced the field for this epic franchise. With a careful balance of challenging facts and accessible content, readers will learn fascinating facts, engage in spirited discussions, and proudly display their Pittsburgh Steelers expertise.

Whether you're a lifelong fan looking to increase your knowledge or a newcomer eager to learn about their storied past, the "Pittsburgh Steelers Fun Facts" book is your go-to source for immersive entertainment.

Read more at www.triviaape.com.

Also by Austin Daniel

Los Angeles Angels: A Profound Journey through Their Illustrious History
Steel City on Skates: The Pittsburgh Penguins' Journey Through the NHL